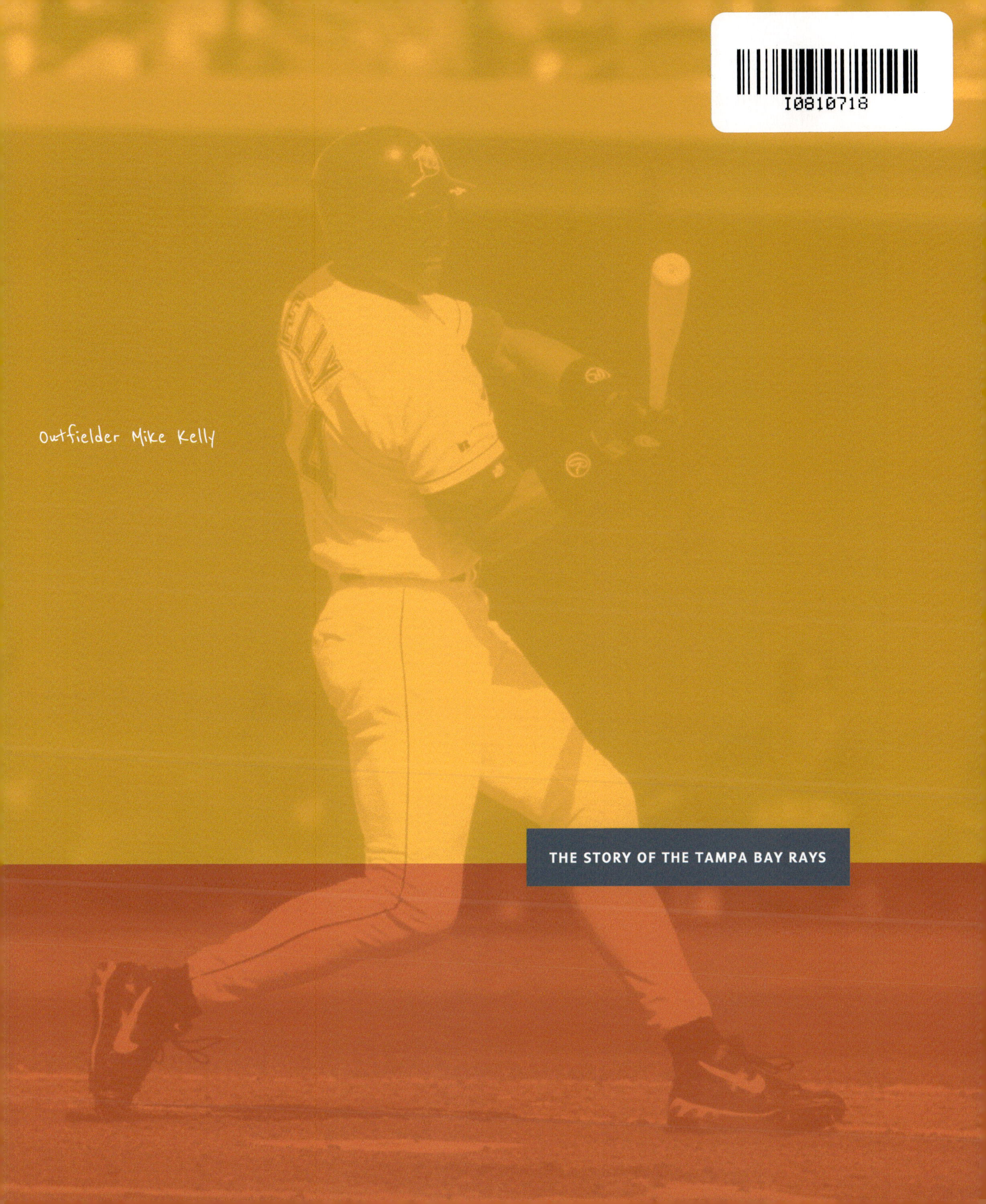

Outfielder Mike Kelly

THE STORY OF THE TAMPA BAY RAYS

Third baseman / First baseman Yandy Díaz

THE STORY OF THE

TAMPA BAY RAYS

JOE TISCHLER

First baseman Fred McGriff

CREATIVE SPORTS

CREATIVE EDUCATION / CREATIVE PAPERBACKS

Published by Creative Education and Creative Paperbacks
P.O. Box 227, Mankato, Minnesota 56002
Creative Education and Creative Paperbacks are imprints of
The Creative Company
www.thecreativecompany.us

Book Design by Wyeth Morgan
Art direction by Blue Design (www.bluedes.com)

Images by Alamy Stock Photo/UPI, 2, ZUMA Press, 25; Getty Images/Alex Trautwig, cover, Brad Mangin, 7 (bottom, left), 11, 18, Chris Bernacchi/Diamond Images, 26-27, Daniel Shirey, 31, David Seelig, 1, 7 (bottom, right), Elsa, 9, J. Meric, 10, 16, Jeff Gross, 6 (bottom, left), Jim McIsaac, 22-23, John Williamson, 3, 19, Kevin C. Cox, cover, 6 (bottom, right), 10, 20, Nick Cammett/Diamond Images, 30, Nick Laham, 15, Otto Greule Jr, 6 (top, right), PETER MUHLY, 4-5, 6 (top, left), 32, Robert Rogers, 12, Ron Jenkins/Fort Worth Star-Telegram, 29, Ron Vesely, 7 (top, right), Tom Pidgeon, 7 (top, left)

Library of Congress Cataloging-in-Publication Data
Names: Tischler, Joe author
Title: The story of the Tampa Bay Rays / Joe Tischler.
Description: Mankato, Minnesota : Creative Education and Creative Paperbacks, [2026] | Series: Creative sports: Major League Baseball | Includes index. | Audience: Ages 8-12 | Audience: Grades 4-6 | Summary: "Discover the Tampa Bay Rays' thrilling journey as they transformed from the Devil Rays, featuring iconic players, unforgettable moments, and the Major League Baseball team's passionate fanbase. Written for middle-grade readers. Includes table of contents, sidebars, and index"—Provided by publisher.
Identifiers: LCCN 2025019584 (print) | LCCN 2025019585 (ebook) | ISBN 9798895811108 library binding | ISBN 9798896800637 paperback | ISBN 9798895812365 ebook
Subjects: LCSH: Tampa Bay Rays (Baseball team)—History—Juvenile literature
Classification: LCC GV875.T26 T57 2026 (print) | LCC GV875.T26 (ebook) | DDC 796.3570975965—dc23/eng/20250607
LC record available at https://lccn.loc.gov/2025019584
LC ebook record available at https://lccn.loc.gov/2025019585

Printed in the United States

Shortstop Kevin Stocker

CANSECO
33

47

CONTENTS

EXTRA INNINGS

TURNAROUND SEASON

The 2008 season was a year of transition for the Tampa Bay Major League Baseball (MLB) franchise. For the first 10 years of its existence, the team was known as the "Devil Rays." It was a rough start for the franchise. Tampa Bay won no more than 70 games in a season. Three times it lost at least 100 games. The Devil Rays finished last place in the American League (AL) East Division 9 of 10 seasons.

The franchise dropped "Devil" from its name prior to the 2008 season. They were now called the Tampa Bay Rays. As usual, the team started out sluggish. But it won seven of eight games at the end of April. For the first time in franchise history, Tampa Bay had a winning record one month into the season (15–12). The Rays continued to win. They held a division lead at the end of May. On August 29, they won their 82nd game of the season. This ensured they would finish the year with their first winning record. Tampa Bay finished with 97 wins. It finished two games ahead of the Boston Red Sox for the AL East title. Amazingly, the Rays were in the playoffs!

Pitcher Matt Garza

EXTRA INNINGS

EVAN LONGORIA
THIRD BASEMAN
RAYS SEASONS: 2008–17
HEIGHT: 6-FOOT-1
WEIGHT: 213 POUNDS
KEY STATS: 2008 AL ROOKIE OF THE YEAR, 3X ALL-STAR, 3X GOLD GLOVE, 342 CAREER HOME RUNS

FACE OF THE FRANCHISE

Evan Longoria came onto the big-league scene early in the 2008 season. He had spent two years in the minor leagues. Team management felt he was ready. Longoria did not disappoint them. He hit .272 with 27 home runs. He notched 85 runs batted in (RBI). He was named AL Rookie of the Year. Longoria truly introduced himself during the playoffs. He hit a total of six home runs against Chicago and Boston. In 2009, Longoria won the first of his three Gold Gloves for his stellar defense. When he left Tampa Bay in 2017, he led the team in games played (1,435), home runs (261), and RBI (892).

Outfielder Rocco Baldelli

In the postseason, Tampa Bay played like a team that had been there before. It beat the Chicago White Sox in the AL Division Series (ALDS) in four games. The Rays met the Red Sox in the AL Championship Series (ALCS). Boston won the first game. Tampa Bay bounced back to win in extra innings in Game 2. It won Games 3 and 4 in Boston to take a 3–1 series lead. The Red Sox won Games 5 and 6 to force a winner-take-all Game 7. The winner would go to the World Series.

Boston scored first on a first-inning solo home run from Dustin Pedroia. It stayed that way until the bottom of the fourth. Rays third baseman Evan Longoria launched a two-out double to right field that scored Carlos Peña from first to tie the game at 1–1. The Rays took the lead in the fifth inning. Willy Aybar led off with a double to left field. Two batters later, Rocco Baldelli hit a single to left to score Aybar and gave the Rays a 2–1 lead. Tampa Bay extended its lead in the seventh inning. Aybar led off with a solo home run to give the Rays a 3–1 lead.

Rays starting pitcher Matt Garza was pitching a gem. He allowed only three hits through seven innings. "I just went out there and emptied my tank and said, 'Hey, here goes, we'll see what happens,'" he said afterward.

BOGGS
12

He was relieved in the eighth inning. Boston loaded the bases. David Price was brought in from the Tampa Bay bullpen. He struck out J. D. Drew to preserve the 3–1 lead.

Price stayed in for the ninth inning. After walking the lead-off batter, he struck out both Mark Kotsay and Jason Varitek. Price retired the last batter on a forceout. The Rays won the AL pennant! The Tropicana Field crowd in St. Petersburg, Florida erupted with joy. After a decade of suffering, Tampa Bay would play in the World Series.

A DEVILISH DEBUT

In the late 1980s, the AL had 14 teams. The National League (NL) had 12. It decided to expand to 14. That way, the leagues would have equal numbers. Ten cities were considered for the new NL franchises. The list was trimmed to six in late 1990. Three were from Florida: Miami, Orlando, and Tampa Bay. The Tampa Bay area consists of two large neighboring cities—Tampa and St. Petersburg—plus several smaller ones. For decades it had hosted MLB teams during spring training. Several MLB teams seriously considered moving to either Tampa or St. Petersburg. They all decided to remain. The area wanted a team of its own. Hoping to improve its chances, Tampa Bay had already built a stadium called the Florida Suncoast Dome (now called Tropicana Field).

The following June, the NL made its selections. It chose Denver, Colorado and Miami. The new teams would begin play in 1993. Four years later, MLB decided to expand again. This time, Tampa Bay was awarded an AL franchise. It would begin play in 1998. The team was placed in the league's East Division.

Third baseman Wade Boggs

The team held a public "name-the-team" contest. The winner was Devil Rays. These creatures are a common sight in Florida waters. The unique fins growing out of their heads resemble horns. The one-of-a-kind Rays Touch Experience at Tropicana Field allows fans to get up close and personal with stingrays, smaller devil ray relatives.

The team took part in a special expansion draft. Then it signed veterans such as hard-hitting first baseman Fred McGriff and third baseman Wade Boggs. It added pitchers Roberto Hernandez and Wilson Alvarez, too. The Devil Rays debuted before a sold-out crowd at Tropicana Field on March 31, 1998. They lost to the Detroit Tigers. McGriff played well all season. Younger players such as second baseman Miguel Cairo and outfielder Randy Winn had solid performances. Still, the Devil Rays finished the year 63–99. They were last in the AL East.

Two veteran players sparked excitement in 1999. Each achieved career milestones. Strapping outfielder Jose Canseco blasted his 400th career home run on April 14. On August 7, Boggs, a Tampa native, became the first major-leaguer to hit a home run for his 3,000th career hit. The Devil Rays were plagued by injuries. But they improved to 69–93.

Tampa Bay fished for some big-name players in the off-season. The Devil Rays thought they caught a big fish when they netted slugging third baseman Vinny Castilla and left fielder Greg Vaughn. Hope quickly evaporated. Slumps and injuries plagued the team. It ended the season with 69 wins again. Tampa Bay dismantled its roster in 2001. That did not help. The team lost 100 games.

Fans cheered for individual performances in 2002. Rookie outfielder Carl Crawford added speed on the basepaths. Third baseman Aubrey Huff led the team with 23 home runs. But the Devil Rays remained at the bottom of the division with an embarrassing mark of 55–106.

THE SLANT AT THE TROP

Tampa Bay's home field of Tropicana Field (nicknamed "The Trop") opened nearly a decade before the franchise began. It was built to lure an MLB team to the area. Before the Devil Rays, the stadium housed the Tampa Bay Storm of the Arena Football League, and the Tampa Bay Lightning of the National Hockey League. The domed stadium may look odd to the viewing public. The stadium's distinct feature is a slanted roof. It was designed to reduce cooling costs on the inside due to the hot and humid Florida summers. It was also built that way to better protect the stadium from hurricanes. In October 2024, powerful Hurricane Milton caused severe damage to the stadium roof. This left the stadium unplayable in 2025.

EXTRA INNINGS

JOE MADDON
MANAGER
RAYS SEASONS:
2006–14

SHIFT AWAY FROM THE NORM

Joe Maddon arrived in Tampa Bay in 2006. It was his first full-time managerial job. He inherited a Tampa Bay club that was still trying to find its way. The team had not come close to a winning season when it started in 1998. Maddon's first two years were rough too. But it all came together in 2008. The Rays remarkably won the AL pennant. Maddon brought in new trends. He was the first manager to extensively use the defensive shift. That is where three infielders would play on one side of the infield. MLB would ban that shift years later. He was also one of the first managers to organize themed road trips. Sometimes he would conduct on-field interviews with birds on his shoulders.

LOU TRIES TO LEAD

Before the 2003 season, the Devil Rays hired Tampa native Lou Piniella as manager. He had led the Cincinnati Reds to the World Series championship in 1990. He also guided the Seattle Mariners to a MLB single season record-tying 116 wins two years prior. "I look forward to the challenge and it's going to be fun," said Piniella. "Managing a baseball team for me is a special privilege, and when you can do it in your hometown, it's even nicer." But Piniella's first year at the helm was not so successful. He had set a goal of 70 wins. The Devil Rays missed that mark by seven games.

In June 2004, Tampa Bay went on a franchise-record 12-game winning streak. But in early July, the New York Yankees put the Devil Rays in their place with a four-game sweep. Then Tampa Bay reverted to its old ways. It won 70 games and finished last in the AL East for the first time.

Tampa Bay took a step back in 2005. They finished in last place with a 67–95 mark. After the season, the team parted ways with Piniella. It hired little-known Joe Maddon to replace him. He was a former bench coach and interim manager for the Los Angeles Angels of Anaheim. The Devil Rays lost 101 games in Maddon's first year. But a crew of young players offered hope that better days were ahead. Crawford ran wild with a league-leading 58 stolen bases. Young pitcher Scott Kazmir emerged as an All-Star.

Maddon was confident he knew how to improve the team. "I believe the biggest thing we have to do around here is we need to change the culture and the way we interact, and our game plan and our concept," he said. "Before we're ever going to win, we have to get that stuff in order."

Pitcher Scott Kazmir

The 2007 season was another learning experience. The Devil Rays finished 66–96. They landed in the basement of the AL East again. Still, good things were happening. Kazmir put up an AL-best of 239 strikeouts. He posted a 13–9 record. Fellow hurler James Shields went 12–8. Tampa Bay also got a boost from veteran first baseman Carlos Peña. He seemed to appear out of nowhere during spring training. He went on to smack a team-record 46 home runs.

STUNNING TURNAROUND

In 2008, players and fans alike witnessed a turnaround season. The team dropped "Devil" from its name. They served notice that they were a team to be reckoned with. The Rays went from worst to first in the AL East. They won 97 games. Maddon was an obvious choice for AL Manager of the Year. This seemingly miraculous improvement was

Left fielder Carl Crawford

EXTRA INNINGS

DAVID PRICE
PITCHER
RAYS SEASONS: 2008–14
HEIGHT: 6-FOOT-5
WEIGHT: 215 POUNDS
KEY STATS: 2012 AL CY YOUNG, 5X ALL-STAR, 2X ERA TITLE, 2,076 CAREER STRIKEOUTS

THE PRICE IS RIGHT

In high school, David Price posted a microscopic 0.43 ERA. The Los Angeles Dodgers drafted him in 2004. Price chose to attend Vanderbilt University instead. He led NCAA Division I colleges in strikeouts his final year. He won several national awards. The Rays made him the top overall pick in the 2007 MLB Draft. His contract included a $5.6-million signing bonus. It was the highest in MLB history. Price played just one year in the minor leagues before coming up to the Rays. He went on to win the AL Cy Young Award in 2012. He also made four All-Star Game appearances while with the Rays.

sparked in part by key additions. Rangy shortstop Jason Bartlett, electric pitcher Matt Garza, and veteran closer Troy Percival joined the team. Rookie third baseman Evan Longoria and speedy young center fielder Melvin Upton Jr. also burst onto the scene.

The Rays beat the Red Sox and White Sox in the AL playoffs. In the World Series, Tampa Bay faced the Philadelphia Phillies. The Phillies eked out a 3–2 win in Game 1. The Rays relied on a strong effort from Shields to win Game 2. Philadelphia took the next three games to capture the crown. The defeat did not stifle the swell of pride in Tampa Bay. "All the negativity has been laid to rest," Maddon said after the season. "We have a bright future ahead of us."

In 2009, Crawford tied the modern MLB record for stolen bases in a single game with six. The Rays began to heat up the following month. Then they hit a rough patch. It derailed their bid to win back-to-back AL East titles. The team finished with its second straight winning mark with 84 victories. But it fell short of the postseason.

Tampa Bay obtained hard-hitting catcher Kelly Shoppach and veteran closer Rafael Soriano before the 2010 season. David Price emerged on the scene as a premier starting pitcher. He went 19–6 with a 2.72 earned run average (ERA). He was runner-up in the AL Cy Young voting. The Rays made another strong surge that year. They edged out the Yankees by a single game to win the division. Their 96–66 record was best in the AL. Soriano had a franchise-record 45 saves. The Rays faced the Texas Rangers in the ALDS. Tampa Bay scored just one run in the first two games at home. It lost them both. The Rays battled back to take Games 3 and 4 in Texas. But the season ended after Game 5. The Rays suffered a 5–1 loss at home. The series made playoff history. It was the first time that the road team won every game.

The following season, Boston was leading the AL East at the end of August. The Yankees were just a game back. Tampa Bay was in a distant third, nine games behind Boston and eight behind New York for the Wild Card berth.

Second baseman / Outfielder Ben Zobrist

RAYS

The Red Sox went into a prolonged slump. The Rays heated up. New York moved into first place. With one game remaining, the Rays and Red Sox were now tied for the Wild Card. The Rays hosted the Yankees. New York carried a 7–0 lead into the eighth inning. Then Tampa Bay exploded. It scored six runs. Longoria drilled a three-run home run as part of the spurt. Dan Johnson tied the game in the ninth on a two-out home run. The game went into extra innings. In the bottom of the 12th inning, Longoria lined a home run down the left field line. Tampa Bay won 8–7. Meanwhile, Boston lost to the Baltimore Orioles. The Rays were in the playoffs! They faced Texas again in the ALDS. The Rays won the opener, but Texas won the next three games to take the series.

STAYING IN CONTENTION

In 2012, Price led the AL with 20 wins and a 2.56 ERA. He won the AL Cy Young Award. Closer Fernando Rodney tallied 48 saves. His 0.60 ERA was the lowest ever by a relief pitcher. The Rays won 90 games. But it missed out on the playoffs.

In 2013, outfielder Wil Myers was called up to the majors in midseason. He played just 88 games. Yet he led all AL rookies with 53 RBI. He was named AL Rookie of the Year. Tampa Bay beat Texas in a tiebreaker game to gain the second Wild Card spot. It then beat the Cleveland Indians in the AL Wild Card (ALWC) Game. But it lost to Boston in the ALDS.

Tampa Bay's string of winning seasons ended the following year. Maddon left. Kevin Cash took over as manager. But three more losing seasons followed.

The Rays returned to their winning ways in 2018. They won 90 games. Left-handed pitcher Blake Snell had a breakout season. After winning just 11

Pitcher Blake Snell

RANDY AROZARENA
LEFT FIELDER
RAYS SEASONS: 2020–24
HEIGHT: 5-FOOT-10
WEIGHT: 185 POUNDS
KEY STATS: 2021 AL ROOKIE OF THE YEAR, 2020 ALCS MVP, ALL-STAR, 11 CAREER POSTSEASON HOME RUNS

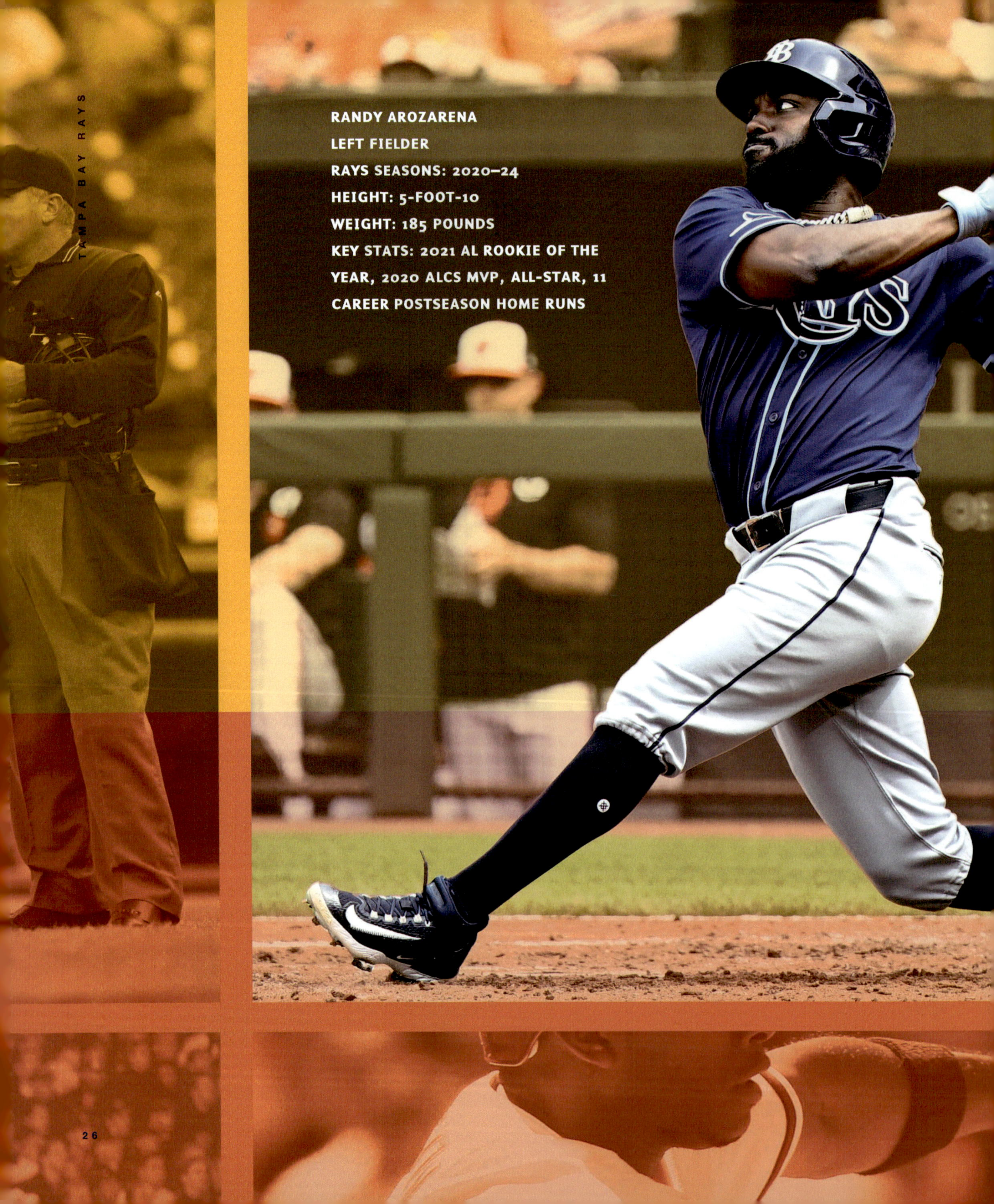

POSTSEASON BREAKOUT

Little was known of Randy Arozarena before the 2020 playoffs. The Rays acquired him in a trade with the St. Louis Cardinals before the season. He had played in only 42 career games before the 2020 postseason. He had eight career home runs. This virtually unknown player would become a household name. Arozarena hit three home runs in the ALDS against the Yankees. He followed that with four home runs in the ALCS win over Houston. He was named ALCS Most Valuable Player (MVP). He added three more home runs in the World Series against the Dodgers. Arozarena set single-postseason records for home runs (10), hits (29), and total bases (64).

games in the previous two years combined, he won an MLB-leading 21 games. He also notched 221 strikeouts and won the AL Cy Young Award. But Tampa Bay missed out on the postseason.

Tampa Bay won 96 games the following season. Snell missed most of the season with an injury. Charlie Morton picked up part of the slack. He won 16 games. It gained a Wild Card berth. The Rays beat Oakland in the ALWC game, 5–1. They then took on a powerful Houston Astros team in the ALDS. The Rays pushed Houston to a deciding Game 5. But Houston prevailed.

The 2020 season was shortened to just 60 games due to the COVID-19 pandemic. Games were played without fans. The Rays started out just 6–8. They followed that start with wins in 11 out of 12 games to take a lead in the AL East. Tampa Bay continued to win. It finished with a 40–20 record. It was the best record in the AL.

The playoffs were expanded to eight teams in each league. The Wild Card series was played at the higher seed. The remaining rounds were played at a neutral site. The Rays hosted the Toronto Blue Jays in a best-of-three ALWC series. Tampa Bay easily swept the series. It moved on to face the Yankees in the ALDS played in San Diego, California. The series went to a deciding fifth game. Mike Brousseau hit a solo home run to break a tie in the bottom of the eighth that gave the Rays a 2–1 lead. Diego Castillo retired the Yankees in order in the ninth.

Tampa Bay faced Houston in the ALCS. The Rays raced out to a 3–0 lead in the best-of-seven series which was also played in San Diego. The Astros battled back to force a Game 7. Randy Arozarena and Mike Zunino each homered to give Tampa Bay a 3–0 after two innings. It would go on to win the game 4–2. The Rays went to the World Series for the second time.

The Rays faced the Los Angeles Dodgers in the World Series played at Arlington, Texas. The two teams split the first four games. But the Dodgers won the next two to take the title.

EXTRA INNINGS

THIRD BASEMAN EVAN LONGORIA (L) AND OUTFIELDER SAM FULD (R).

BACK-TO-BACK DO-OR-DIE

Tampa Bay finished the 2013 season tied with Texas for the second wild card spot in the AL. A tiebreaker game was needed. The winner moved on to the playoffs. The loser's season was done. It was played in Texas. The Rays ace, David Price, was the starter. He threw a complete game in the Rays 5–2 win. Two days later, Tampa Bay was on the road for another do-or-die game. This was the AL Wild Card Game at Cleveland. Four Rays pitchers kept Cleveland off the scoreboard. The Rays won 4–0. Tampa Bay moved on to the ALDS. Its momentum would end there though. Boston beat Tampa Bay in four games.

Pitcher Shane McClanahan

Tampa Bay won a franchise-best 100 games in 2021. Arozarena batted .274 with 20 home runs. He was named AL Rookie of the Year. The Rays met Boston in the ALDS. Tampa Bay shut out the Red Sox 5–0 in Game 1. Boston's bats woke up in the next game. It won 14–6. The Red Sox won the next two games in Boston to take the series.

Tampa Bay earned Wild Card berths the next two seasons. But it lost in the ALWC series both years. The Rays finished with a losing record of 80–82 in 2024. It marked their first losing season in seven years.

In October 2024, powerful Hurricane Milton blew through the Tampa Bay area. It caused major damage to Tropicana Field. Much of the roof was destroyed. The stadium was deemed unplayable for the 2025 season. The Rays moved their home games to the Yankees spring training complex in Tampa.

Tampa Bay baseball fans have been a patient group. They waited more than 80 years for their own major-league team. Then they endured a decade of losing seasons before experiencing success. The Tampa Bay faithful continue to throw their support behind the Rays. Soon they may see a world champion rise up by the bay.

Third baseman Junior Caminero

INDEX